THE EXIT SHOW

Books by Anne F. Walker

Poetry

Into the Peculiar Dark
Pregnant Poems
Six Months Rent

Anthology Edited

bite to eat place

THE EXIT SHOW

Poems

Anne F. Walker

National Library of Canada Cataloguing in Publication Data
Walker, Anne F.
The Exit Show
ISBN 0-9733952-0-6
I. Title — Poetry
9 780973 395204

Thank you: Canada Council for the Arts; Ontario Arts Council; Dawn Marie Kresan for investing in bringing more poetry into the world; Andrea Rosati & Margo Ponce & Wendi Robbins & Andi Wolf for workshop support; Bob Acker for repeatedly asking for this manuscript; Solomon Kent Ireland for reading it so carefully; Peter Darbyshire & Paul Savoie for making my Toronto literary world a friendlier and happier place; Benny Rietveld for the righttimerightplacepep-talk; Alfred Arteaga, Hertha D. Sweet Wong and Lyn Hejinian for such positive and integral support at Berkeley; and always and so much Jamil.

Some of these pieces have previously appeared as follows: "thatnightclickthing" section of "The Exit Show" first appeared in *The Malahat Review*; "not santa anas" and "train wreck in a woman" first appeared in separate issues of *Queen Street Quarterly*; "Enter the Apartment" first appeared in *Grain*; "Orange trim you finished painting as labour began" first appeared in *Contemporary Verse 2*; "and the sun sets (throat-bright)," "(no matter where i travel i'm still writing you (poems))," "(no matter where i travel i'm still writing you (poems))," and "thread of comment," first appeared in *Zugernat*; "For July" first appeared in *Canadian Dimensions*; "Pink String" first appeared in *Santa Clara Review*; "1/11" appeared in *The New Delta Review*, and in *poetrysuperhighway.com*; "eclipse," "One," "Leaving You Sleeping," first appeared in *the muse apprentice guild*; and "seduction" first appeared as "addiction" in *Janus Head*.

A selection of poetry from *The Exit Show* was shortlisted for the K.M. Hunter Artist Award through the Ontario Arts Council. *The Exit Show* manuscript won the Eisner Prize for Poetry at the University of California, Berkeley, 2002.

from and for

andrea

CONTENTS

THE POETICS

NEXT

THE POETICS

Hands the size

everytime i see you it feels tentative. i'm sure it's a one-nighter.

everytime i'm not sure if you will still fit me, height to my height

the small room   adjacent to the kitchen from which you feed me night after night where the
        nights

are never sequential. often months apart. but no time between. as if each of us has travelled
        light years.

returned to the same spot un-aged. your face is still and eyes hold gaze

still as i have ever seen. // you undo me. when i look at you i hold nothing:

a woman in hot spring pools, letting the postures of my imagination present themselves and
        leave

placed on the rocks, thoughts springboarding off the other couples and singles who populate.
        i imagine i know them, and then do not.

i imagine i know you. and then do not.

footnote 21. recognition. couples and who they are in bipartite equations, routines, the blonde 36 year old Marin doctor's wife who looks 21, her slim strip and dance routine by the pool, with muñequita, pat's wife. pat all buff upstairs in the kitchen smoking in the kitchen smoking and. we look down to the hot tub spa. muñequita moves and sits naked on the thin edge. a woman with beautiful brown store-bought breasts puts an orange-red plastic lobster between muñequita's shaved legs, over her shaved lips. pat upstairs shouts now you've got crabs. laughs.

start sequence 8. selling a car

a glide of space above a boxy red jeep cherokee beneath
a white heron slides through air above freeway next to
(you were a bird. you were) next to the estuary

those constant small motions, of the series of docks
in which your boat is tethered, begin to suggest
how delicately (to me briefly, you were the ocean

start sequence 1. buying a car (because beauty is where it can be touched)

its crush-brown side reminds
       me of your slide eye
the way it changes shape on the right.
drives clean as a man biting
the back a woman's neck

(feel those insecurities
click clack crawling like metallic
spiders over a glass globe

shudder over you

last time it was rain & flood

The house is safe when I'm in it

she dreams

he dreams of developing a language of which he can only use fragments

     but those convey meaning so poignantly

she dreams again of a house on a hill, glass overlooking

     the ocean. This time the waves are contrived but still

     overwhelm the house

         now a smaller version of the house, lit up on twin peaks, the indoor pool and spa overlooking the bay, in s.f. @ the sex party for short, Mardi Gras beads made of small gold dice slip't off in the i ndoor pool. The musician with beading shining curling hair watched like a Long Island mechanic at a sex club watched grrrls glam-glossed like calendar pages. & it's something to do with anxiety.

I'm in a symbolic landscape with you.

it's about sex

you say

     I'm in a symbolic landscape. I am a Georgia O'keeffe painting. I am an open flower you pull legs together tight lips and open flower. I'm watercolours and oils.   I'm internet pictures and voices with whom you correspond.   I'm the multitude at   PleasureZone.   The one woman in short black dancing for her lover at the pole.   Him watching her like possession, angry and desperately needing exactly what she gives him with the other women on stage.   No other man would dare touch her.   I'm in my body again and feeling.   You smell like heat and sleep.   You call me a lullaby.   You crack chiropractic my back / call out my flexibility ~ *say it's easier with uptight women, they crack easily, hold tight* easily.   You show me your pictures of women, flicker screen to screen.   Warren. Worn already.   You seem.   To defy time.

it's about sex
you say

start sequence 2. in its imperfection

see the stone patio café in the zocalo again its

high-mountain-dry and smoggy-in-the-small-streets and

the thin lank-haired man 8 years older than me

my step-granny (12 years older than he, Esperanza)

ska'd him away like a dog with a tsss and

that *beauty is in its imperfection* which he'd said before he ran

like a skat-flicked-wrist and that

that sentence

stuck in my head and in the rose garden today i see that it

/ *that beauty is* / in nearness not in

any ideal of form that takes itself / like a Ming vase never to be touched / but in the

intimate grasp / the imperfection of any ideal separated from abstract by touch. or by

breath,

and that slight-off i bought today: it revels your beauty.

NEXT

(no matter where i travel i'm still writing you (poems))

we make each other more real. a small room we share in vancouver, in new orleans
i am the fork and you the silver knife
on the red cotton table cloth
on the edge of the french quarter
by the gulf / of an ocean
broad as the unnamed between
(no matter where i travel)
— i'm still writing you poems

(no matter where i travel i'm still writing you (poems))

we make each other more real. i am the fork and you the silver spoon

we make each other more real. i am the fork and you the silver knife

we make each other more real. like a small room we share in oakland, our things everywhere

      on the wall after

nine years in prison for you and six for me but that's the way these things

play out. we took her to the restaurant and i biked to her home and yes, i came inside

(and no matter where i travel my love)

— i'm still writing you poems

thread of comment

For over a year I would turn on my computer in the morning for the thought of you

and that led me down the charcoal maze corridors of the underground

travelled toward some centre, some half man half beast in the centre

I would think about the letters you wrote me and reread them over and over, check

in the morning again, and you were still there. For over a year I imagined ways to find your
        city

and live there. Over the year that became more frail and dream-like, the body-heat you brought
        my mind

less and less to occasional and now a job in Montreal and that's still not close enough

because you already said, 'I can't really talk, she's here.'

Last night there was an apartment with two rooms, bunkbeds in the main room and I didn't see
        the bedroom because you were in it with her

and wouldn't open the door. You had two roommates and the place became a ship,

there were exciting shiny people coming and going, your queer foreign roommate flirted with
        me genuinely because he saw my pain and need.

When you finally emerged it was with an absence of recognition of all that had just passed. You
        were caring

and thoughtful and refused to feel with me. We walked through a plaza where a pathway led
        down in a U-shape. You led us down

and the fountain that dissected the path in half didn't leave enough room and we both became
        wet and all along I wanted it to be like Vancouver.

I wanted to feel like we had each flown thousands of miles just to see one another.
I kept feeling happy with you and forgetting that you were hers and this was your gesture of
        civility, or your first infidelity,
kept feeling those same pleasures that had haunted me from you over and over a year and
        everywhere there were people watching us (commenting and)
enjoying their view.

water-skitters

so there i am crossing through the hood, door lock't, on my way to the pediatrician to get the sweet small one some inhaled steroids to knock this bout of asthma out (the albuterol isn't cutting it and it's just got to be knock't all down before it gets chronic), and just before i get there to telegraph i see this awesome image. breath stopped. i see it through wire mesh fence that lines the crossing of the car bridge above the images of the BART trains. it appears like at least seven freeways' floating skyramps intersect. i can't even imagine. it must be the 24, the 580, the 380, and what?...the 80 perhaps is separate there? maybe a street off- or on- ramp? but there they all were crossing and separating out each other like leaves in some surreal futuristic flower set in wire fences and against some surreal sky.

(which i now hand to you)

flaca

the morning after telling me you did heroin at the speedway

while we cooked through wine like dregs

you told me the cornfield

out back / was mown down in like ten / it startled you.

there it was, silk all yellower than summer hair, then a machine ditched it

in less time than it took to make a coffee and pop some ibuprofen.

Orange trim you finished painting as labour began

Things slip by.
A huge man past the kitchen
window. The shoulders and jacket
dark
        as light on a highway so bright
it's invisible
        and slips through eyes and molecules
lips and hands
        while we speak and whisper
and the baby sleeps.

And that slips by
unmarked
like everything else

(past the kitchen window
        and

through the outside brick

for July

legs that come out in Summer
like pale celery stalks

& a mother who says again quietly
                    to herself
              in the bathroom's
         morning damp
    I'll write that down one day.
But now I have just to breathe
ease into this one new day's shapeless bulk
unafraid.

two archangel numbers:
retail slut

Startled by her: the first time it was winter: he was one side a counter and she the other. He going, in his grey wool wrap, back to a project sponsored by grief. Across a machine. She looks at him and he registered that, went on through days and nights like a tunnel under a lush hillside a tunnel through which he might hold his breath and wish at the top of a long street. And he remembered her eyes. All he could think was they were so dark and soft brown any language to describe them would be prosaic; the poetry was about her use of them. He felt truly seen although he had then turned back into the tunnel of his difficulties without looking back walked through the cafe door into muted winter morning light.

     The second time was spring. He was fresh from swimming saw her and they at the same time spoke. The same words and stopped, twice. So she says 'jinx' like a kid and he turned away blushing. The air suddenly flesh or water he could turn in with an overhand stroke and leave behind history. It shocked him that he turned from her, reminded him how easy it is to age inside a mind, to become spidery and frightened. The third time she's across a room and to him lit it like a lighthouse beam. But he was with his father: which paralysed him.

He didn't know if he'd see her again but they end up with a month. She turns out to be the kind that's good at flings. Good at the speed and intensity and impossibly frightened by the ragged sway that their connection brought forward. Over his kitchen table in the house that overlooked the bridge that lead to the city she says 'why is this so hard? Why is all this coming up?' She feels guilty for cancelling on him two nights running. She feels that he was always criticising her. She feels like he just wants sex with her, doesn't take her school or thinking seriously. That he treats her like a slight thing in a broken frame. He thought perhaps there was more she felt guilty for, a reason for her absence that she didn't describe. He felt more raw and up against it then than he could remember. He felt like a punk-rocker at a club, arms bear, poetry in hand, waving his voice into the air, he leaned in across the plank table and said, 'because there is something happening. If there was nothing happening between us neither of us would care and it would just be light.

She asks if he will be in later that night, he asked why, she says 'so we can make plans for tomorrow.' Then the tomorrow was tense and hard. They ate at an Ethiopian restaurant, she says the other one down the street had a better atmosphere, but it was more expensive and she'd been there a few days before. He thought slowly 'with who?' while she was talking about studying animal consciousness at school: she looks at him and says, 'no one can know what another sentient being is thinking. . .   I mean, we're sitting here and really, we have no idea what the other is thinking.' He felt silenced and nodded.

She falls away with a few phone calls but won't plan to see him again. He didn't try tha hard: he knew the cafe she worked every day and that when he crossed her path physically she responded. He didn't go in. He wrote poems for her she would never read.

Marriage

I met you at the café. You eating spinach salad. You said it looked good and I thought you
meant something about me and you meant the greens scattered with red seeds. I couldn't eat
or drink anything. Talked to you about cities, invisible cities you had been unable to use. I
watched you eat the seeds one by one left on your plate; month after month you consumed,
some cross-dressed Persephone at Odyssia, married to this culture, married to nothing to do
with me. We talked about the McArthur BART. We talked about the planes and freeway,
the clouds. You talked about the city rushing around everyone and everyone oblivious (*the guy
on the cell phone who could have been anywhere,* you said, *if you can just say something about
the experience of the city.* You picked those seeds from the plate. I wanted to ask for one,) but
I wasn't, (I didn't.) You talked about moving to a city this side of the bay, that it would mean
you'd get a car. Then you'd have to find parking. I left without eating or drinking
and for the first time, felt the lightness of leaving. Home packed
already, and nothing to tie me here.

start sequence 3. confessions 3958

i blew a doll. you're a doll. up there behind the bar
i gotta free coffee off today (from some woman) you
ducked away

an object. sells objects
in the store. like you, in the store
the 2 men following both have that short
sexual-predator haircut, and new piercings and a smooth
dissatisfied intolerance, mixed with hungry and smooth
under the motions of (the) skin

you were the wake-up. that kind of scud
between dream and waking, you were sets of twos.

silent poem instructions

go up market girl. to the free way and
(so like this nation i loved the drive here
pass the bay and docks michael
lives near the curve current
the freeway away the intersect
like flower petals for peter)
and you're home.

i lasso the moon for you
and all you say is 'so?'

  didn't sleep
through the day at all today
some coffee with andrea and felt that rise
not linked to addiction.
some little pale
earlier without it. but i was already
            stoned on her
and all the nettles that brings

it's very important to watch the open sky tonight
no blinds on the window, the city's writing (in) the dark

or the bright from those clouds.

San Andreas Fault

Zero is minus 20 Celsius,

or something like that. I don't

want to see you. I've seen you

naked as a starfish, naked in a nest of seven like

you've seen me in a three

that same night that night

in a house of flesh, I've seen

your bare voice each night

the other end my phone

your dailies appeared and we spoke and spoke and she

and she and she

One

> *it's that when the beautiful butterflies flicker by i become one*
> *briefly with them. and i could not metamorphise with her*
> *this time*

I missed the meteor shower of the lifetime
 yesterday. I missed your call. You
 were always exploding anyway.
A shut click lock door wall window wall.
 Body clear, and air lit like through heat
one is seen the other side a bon-fire
moving slow(ly) in its light
 The air moulds differently around one alone
One. One. One. One.
 One. I can't care. One. there is no
Progression. One. The Same Air. One. The
same place.
 One. You call. One. You are always
exploding.

Seduction

start it out normal: girl-2 follows into the hotel in which

the conference was held

calls back to girl-1's car. names like stones.

i had walked like a star. i felt like a star.

we walked after lunch, after i took off and replaced my sweater enough to call attention

to the animal print tank top to my body

which has lost weight with this illness.

we walked and shopped for our children. i tour guided

guided through the city more like through memories

this is not that city i left. i am not the girl who left. despite remnants / of architectures.

in the swank art bar my divorced husband

first took me to. a first date (or second.) (first

we drink red wine and smoke canadian cigarettes

and then in a comedy of bad directions we stumble

into girl-a and girl-b's apartment only set to pace

quick minnows glitter click in a thick slow as molasses cold

against girl-a and girl-b's stillness and weight: punk-girls,

inert as heroin, in mourning. and my apologies and keys returned

and the steps each tighter to find the bed

we clutch into. i into each of you. one a voice

one a mouth. both so focused. i want so hard to promise /

never to forget (you, like coffee in an upscale smoke-bar in the pricey part of town,

like leather, and a movie about to flicker on

temporal

the presence
of a body that turns like a hand
on a clock
in open pace with my own that turns

you are the hour
i the minute.

chiasmus

actually the three siblings weren't all that awful. there was the one hot one, with a grace in his self, but he was kin, and no matter how married-in, kin is kin and not to be gone there with. the first step-sister was exacting; the second, kind. (the parents had never been particularly or regularly attentive, always lost in foreign countries or books.) but still cinderella had to keep up the house; and that is a task, day after day after day. one day, a magic faery—one who was only to be found in the slip between two opposing currents of wind, where one soul becomes light in the embrace of another—appeared briefly and gave cinderella a chance to buy leather knee-high boots that made her little retro-satin-black dress fit to be worn again, particularly with the purple feather boa. cinderella left the brother and the sisters at home. much as you can ever leave kin behind.

cinderella dressed her cousin in red plush, in rhinestones and a little slip of black vest and took the boots and the dress and the boa and her cousin and her cousin's husband, both from the inner valley, her village friend and that friend's boyfriend, and that friend's boyfriend's roommate who the village friend had wanted to set up with cinderella (like some resonance of a line behind a golden goose peeling in from some other story), and cinderella's stylin' glitter-pal. all together she took them to this party the prince had invited her to when they had met briefly at the café, just days after cinderella had received the gift of the boots. the prince's dance hall was wild. music perfect and all cinderella's posse danced and danced and danced except the cousin's husband who was one who was still in his body in some way. he watched his wife like love. maybe like something else too, a bit flatter, more grey and heavy like perfect skipping stones or the thick low floor of rainclouds over raised even farm-lands between mountains.

glitter girl was the first to notice that, as the handsome young prince changed CDs, he held to his face a feather shed from cinderella's purple boa. of course she pointed it out to the whole posse. the prince seems to gravitate through the night. cinderella's cousin vidies the situation and says to herself *well if i don't set this like a clock in motion this time will skip by like others have* and decided to leave that little slip of a hour-glass black vest—a bit retro 70s with its somewhat wide lapel and just a little tiny bit on the goth side—on the wood bench of the dance hall. as she lived in the inner valley she could certainly not come out herself to get it. of course, cinderella would have to.

look, i'm not saying there were any glass slippers involved, or that the shattering of any syntax is really necessarily connected to romantic love. that may just be café talk: or not. those things may have broken in any number of divorces, on the dance floor, under the couch after they had been kicked off for the dance (of) all night; or they may not have. they may come into a different story. all i'm saying is that the handsome prince emailed cinderella: *Sin*, he says *the top is in my kitchen, so i can pass it on at your convenience.* he sure seemed polite for a handsome prince.

Medea
(sewing)

eyes like blue grapefruit sections.
i don't really need much
sleep or food much
anymore.

a slim ridge on either side
of your spine
and hips like dragon teeth
            or (butterfly) wings.

Leaving You Sleeping

Each time I see that worn
blue and white hockey shirt
slanted up over your shoulder.

It's cold here.
You sleep shirted
under blue watercolour sheets
and spread
your body in odd distortions.

Still asleep,
you turn as I touch the door,
thicken lips to hush me.

London (for Andrea)

cars scoot by soundlessly,
i wonder how you are

also in snow,
the storm from Texas

probably up in the air
around you   and her

yours is an opal vein in overlapping off-angel plates of black slate
a route through a continent i can not cross

even though desire might
pave that wide road.

Archangel again

hot and dry the days before christmas. you are the day of the
night of the full moon where the moon was closest to earth 130
years each direction. the earth close too to the sun. the brilliance.
and you called in the wash of light; the bare winds up all day and
night. i couldn't sleep anyway~

Enter the apartment

I   .

the dark room, the sparse living room in the small military
apartment. After the child has been put to sleep and the late
guests given tea and conversation, a hug at the door. The small
light in the bedroom comes on. The slim grey computer four
years out of date whirs on. There's a message sent: two names
and no text between: it's the middle of the night *each name a rising
or setting sun*, absence articulating presence like an echo, how
close hands come before feeling the heat or gravity of the other.
He already deep under and heavy, a weighted back; she thick
with wine and flirtation, just need touch him. Just need know he's
there

I   I   .

this month the bills came in like rain. it's a slim roof we've built of
loans. i've described this house before. its likeness to all the
others. its creaking and neighbours not far enough to offer
silence. i wonder if i don't feel the pain yet which is to wash over
me. i wonder if i have spent on you what should have been
saved.

train wreck in a woman

Some men get excited by a train wreck in a woman.

I think you are one.

The way your mother spilt that coffee on your face and neck that were covered
        by some wool cloth, you'd had a cold i think, home sick from school, in a
        room of women drinking coffee poured from a silver percolator in the 1950's
        you attempt to glamorise

ineffective in your argument / the wool particularly

leaving a small scar on your neck the woman touched in Chiapas, she always
        wanted the revolutionaries you told me. you told me you told her it was a
        scar you got in the revolution and she touched it and you until you told it
        was not true. you told me.

maybe it offended you i wouldn't take your offer of wine and comfort

but instead chose not to crash

leaving the small scar on your neck i had touched outside Odyssia when our
        bodies before parting again moved like spoons, then with five feet of air
        between, you had told me there and then about the scar, pretending it had
        been from a revolution: and i knew you were lying.

you asked me how i knew 'n you told me about the woman touched in Chiapas,
        she'd always wanted the revolutionaries you told me. all the men hated her
        you told me you told her it was a scar you got in the revolution and she
        touched it and you until you told it was not true. you told me /

ineffective in your argument / you accused me / and maybe / it offended you i wouldn't
     take your offer of wine and comfort
but instead chose not to crash

i knew you were lying

Date: Tue, 29 May 15:58:47 PDT

From: randomchaos@ pleasantville.muse

To: gate_angel@hotmail.whitescreen

Subject: weather channel

> "so bloody tired up here..."

> like a universal state spreading across a city or territory? rather
than humidity there is tired in the air. thick all over the walls of
buildings. hospitals look one dimensional. plants thrive in it of
course, but sometimes it makes tempers flare. the occasional drive-
by...naturally...which the police say is tired-related. "it's the season,"
they say, "that's all. in a few months it will shift to the chipper
season and we'll all be skiing...whistling. no need for alarm."

SNOW SUITE

Christmas Poem: a little *thing* going

gotta, gotta/gotta drink more fluids

gotta watch less t.v. gotta/gotta

get some romance have a few good shits

gotta celebrate

gotta celebrate christmas gotta

drink more fluids. find some rest somewhere

in this bed and arms   i don't know

with slasher films played and replayed

multi-deadly daily.

/

and i'm thinkin'   where's the love poetry?

and i'm thinkin'

when she arrives he/you become whole again

I.

There is a car   there waiting: like a used condom in a box in a bag
                                            he carries from the room in his brother's house:
like a house full of intimate family.

He tried to hush me in bed last night.
Snow flying like bees around a hive.
I feel emotional oscillation then link
your fingers all wiggle like my toes
wrapped up around your back while i'm rapt in
you rapt in you like the open eyes' eyes are to the video-game
in the next-room-living-room the video-game moves
into the open eyes' mind and nerves go off
like a body stretched into a star turned
on three moving metal spheres in a
streetfair in San Francisco on Easter
Sunday (*the cult of death* Marxist-Charlie
calls that—

your fingers all move separately, slide as if peeling many
cellophane experiential layers simultaneously *onion-skin bible peel* wrestling
documentary *peel* sterile

family highway travel in a rental car (heat-air chap-dry) *peel*
this place peelslightlypeel the air the way windows shut to light

(to the biting cold).

The snow clots the sky.

(You pull sleeping bags and an air (gag) mattress
and bags and backpacks toward the waiting car)
and Amanda arrives.

hummingbird and Last Night

'i'm a humming bird' he says at
        the carlton centre plaza underground
        closed on sunday
we look out three story slant plate glass
        windows across a skate rink
        where a few kids and parents (moms) move
'and you are the flower i skip back
        to'
        'sweet sweet flower' he descends into
        old man mutterings and grabs my thigh

and the night begins to sail open and wide
        at 2 a.m.
and i'm wondering why i read him (as) unsure.

and the sun sets (throat-bright)

feather-blue the sky is feather-blue
against the bare orange branches this cycle of this moon

i can't sit with this weight
a peach pit apricot pit some sore mouth

does she offer these gifts to everyone?
or is it you

alone?

falling fast
(after paul's poem)

       all the loops of thought
       spiral small and smaller,
       a decaying orbit, an archaic
       radio broadcast, his master's
       voice tilting the dog's head,
       an old l.p. skuttering to its
       centre

       and the song is over
       and two face each-
       other in silence

       my soul turns when i see you
       simple as that.

like Bach's Concerto in A minor

1.

i have all this stuff to keep me company,
papers that need to be sorted, short
relationships like passages that each need check-ins
and outs. busy work. and you still the world
and all the small sounds of industry
and i hear what's beneath.

2. River Poems

we were so drunk we
        were swimming deep under a
        dark rippled stream
two silver fish. one guiding. one
        coming up for air. i was
        gagging. you unclean
        your hands
smell like another woman

(like a throat)

when the slip appears a throat disk a
        river stone flat as slate
        eyes like you
i get under it.

each encounter

is a boat out into a stream,

water calm and fast and chilling-

ly cold and sun and air hot and barely

fear / of any other side

or toppling. your hands are so strong.

3. who hasn't yet hush

you remind me that i want him

probably like i remind you of a wife

      blurred behind years away from each other

finding each other in letters and rare phone calls

sharing history and distance and absence and here

i am, new to you and you new too

even though something long about your body

is like him, the tattoo is different but equal:

a sun on right shoulder rather than dragon

on shin and abstracts on the lower back

your skin soft like he

who never kept me.

even though she knows

it's a hollow ruthless little hole
we've carved out of the week, on this afternoon
(or that) always changing always
a time she is at work
and it's just sex but it's never just sex it's
a reminder that the flesh comes open and naked that
desire is new and separate from (social) meaning
it's you pull your legs in and i give over
and over until i'm through
and exhausted
and it's time to go

it's not the book i thought i'd write it in either

this day i went the other way on market

the man with his 3 dogs and 2 shopping carts together the girl

in the car. in the white car. the man holds a bike 1 hand

garbage bags the other to guide the carts the dogs pull,

the pigeon ruffed up. And You're in your kitchen.

that wasn't the poem i thought i'd write. i thought it'd be about

the way your mouth tastes like meat or salt, that

the poem the way you read it

was unrecognisable

and / laid out in your bed, your wife's bed

and you reading Sappho (that one that ends in shudder, in death), and never

will i hear that unrecognisable

again

and you reading Sappho (that one that ends in shudder, in death), and never

vancouver: peter in a hotel room

there is that drop-off zone i go all shark-eyed
and i want to know
if it's true. and if it's not
let it drop away.

so... angel-at-the-gates-of-heaven / slide some hand my way sugar~

hear some music filling up the room. *the cd's off.* it wakes up the animal print on the sofa. opens the space between objects and circulates as if the balcony door was open and winds blowing in. *radio's off.* the brown judo mat flat. *no tape* no song in the air. but hear it. *call you*

and there is a tunnel made in the sky, like some matrix in which gravity is absent to allow one thing to pass to another, planets to shift orbit to another sun, a plane to cross a continent. like the blind raising in the old apartment a crow flies through the courtyard, hollowing space around its wings, pushing the air back, a story that moves beyond the perimeters of imagination.

unlearn the travels off your back

read your body slow as a map
on which i trace the lines
to where we meet.

Education in America

Categorizing the what is allowed the speak don't speak, be free & freely
refrain your unauthorized thoughts

Don't look into the void too deeply or
the void is looking back already
                  consume you
                  swallow you

small sequence

2

like the man in the 1/2 moved room said

in our case if you'd let go the colossal load of closing

you seem to carry, let go the social conventions, like hinges in a door

i was always trying to open. you

   to shut. my foot got stuck

i was trying to sell

ideas, ways of approaching, bare bits of

   poems embedded in a city like

a man 'n a woman

where the woman saw the man

   in a telegraph eatery

       and changed the direction   of everything

          just to speak to him

and he acted like he barely noticed

except for those very tight hinges, those

            social conventions

where he appeared light, then froze

     solid as Dante's Lucifer

waist-deep in the stuff of his surroundings

governing his world / from his immobility.

Buckled: i rolled and woke

the horizon waved as if in heat as if
in an aftershock as if the air
was the skin of water that had
a pebble drop't in

learning for leaving

Archangel walks me around
the Emeryville marina and it was the

moon eclipsing the sun and the
position of planets it was a seal he'd seen
the day before / the ocean
chatter about Canada and schools and piercings and him learning
boats (that will take him) and those eyes
that leave me wasted.

eclipse

washing dishes in front of the window when the eclipse at last began. hands wet, glass between she and the outdoors; a mud-veil of cloud, in and out, over the moon. "i don't know, i was drunk a lot that year, it was a good year, a lot of parties," the hourglass neighbour said about the last eclipse, ten years before, as they all gathered, children peering into the thick white telescope on the balcony, other children walking loud through the courtyard. the moon half re-lit: the man moved uncomfortably, as if to adjust something technical, laughing a little too much. his wife barer then than he preferred.

it's a (hot) prickly thick heat all day

been dry and crooked today
turned away from a kiss you woke me
while i walked a long road
dirt road in the dark kind of night
when you can't see your own hand and
no stars light the sky and
the soft heat of the earth
is almost sponge

Exit the Apartment

thread the eye with my body.

I haven't seen you in months. And then it was an accident as you pandered

to an ugly powerful woman in a café by work. I had

barred you from seeing

me. My hands let loose, filled with something cold in you I could not see

you and ride out you

in another's bed with any

particular grace. And now I plunge back through you as you

sew, gentle as a machine,

your next leaving

Onetwotwoonetwotwo

stand at san quentin's gate at midnight
protesting the murderer's murder while
the life of gem's sister
unexpectedly seeps away to a cancer
that started as pressure behind her
eyes.
How could you not protest death itself
dispersing after midnight, arm around
gem and a weight barely bridged as you span
the san rafael skyway home
through the toxins of richmond
to cosy bricked berkeley cosy cosy here.

Fridge-note left over from that that marriage

Remember this. I am always in the basement.
No matter how swank the parlour you become able to afford or
the language you speak — country you live in. No matter if your house has no basement built-i
I am always in it. It is cold
and base heated and concrete painted red and shadows painted on one wall. I am always in it
like a ghost bricked into your psyche.
The purple cloth will sway in the wind raising goose pimples in the wet flesh. I am always in
wearing sweats and masturbating in front of a
t.v. waiting for you to pinch my flesh and remember
the fabric and swing like a pit toward the centre the centre line.
Come wrestling for me in the pit.

STAR-LIT SUITE

beauty in chaos

                              in a room
                        with a bone and dirt
                  and waterstained cracked
                        walls

                                          balcony stuffed, scuffed with
                        wood bits, and poles so you can't
                        walk out without
                        risking slipping

three stories from the Victorian
        attic

grasping in downtown sky
    scrapers into your
        eyes' last vision.

                  Pink string winds
                  up into the sharp sky - where singing
                  harpstrings strung star to star
                  keep honey from sticking to
                  a suburban mouth.

You smoke drugs named little blue pills

on cigarettes to chase away gargoyles
from the mirror's other side.
They frighten. You smoke ground
candy-blue coating and white fire-soft,

a bag of pure ego.

And you listen with the calm of a lifelong
patient
told not to do.

Earth and sky meet.

Beauty is a painted egg, or a honeycomb of apartments at dusk,
broken plates of light, wood bowl darkness thrown out an
        upstairs window,
  back alley milkcrates and boxes that had contained fruit,
or the high pitch squeal
like a radio off-station

                  that recedes you from numbness
     still feel

sweet of imperfection

so

beautiful you have to stay up till dawn - eating rubbery microwave
warmed bagels and cream cheese underneath a buzzing air duct -
each day, just to understand, or cry, or see it start allover.

3   both nights dreams of circuitry. first falling through another country.
         the small turns and balances. toward one two years past. today
         through the sharp edges of a blocked spine psyche, where turns are
repetitions   held open mouth, hand over eyes. he wraps her up and holds her and
         holds her and holds her. like three turns consecutive, finally moving
         the fourth direction.

                       8

there's something about doing weights
the slow wait the MRI / hours
the phone rings the music played the
days locked in with you. tapping.
a tunnel of sequential nights. tapping
a fallen man on the hollow trunk
        of his body.

12

how can it be that i am here and there
a waiting room (zippers) a woman smiled and
others come and go / the room's arch / my arms
up over my head / your mouth just above
nipple / your holding me / people coming and going
walking thru / you / say you want to make sure
i stay for a long time

13

move thru the world differently than most
less anchored than most — the world spins
and watch it dissolve and replace
like a series of questions

repetitions. there's something about the long laid out fuck with you the sound in the MRI / the clicking / first / the exploratory. the loud sound like jackhammering muted by plastic earphones in which my own music plays softly too softly, i wish that it would blare like bad religion october 7th 2000 at the warfield // wash away /// wash away all the fears that wiggle out my toes wash away her and her putting me away wash away the fear that wraps me like the inside body of a worm. the MRI echoing. echolocation like those submarine sailors drown by their own need for air and their nation's too proud to ask for help. drown like the air coming and going in the small light casket of the MRI, drown like i can't think of you / drown like the way i have to keep my hands close in not to feel the parameters of the small space bound like a child wrapt tight and closeted for crying. bound like fear that comes, wakes / places, moves and does not escape. breathing and breathing. that's all it is or can be sometimes. breathing.

i just keep wanting to see you / just so i know what it's not

9

perimeters

parameters

15

you flickers quick as glitters

i didn't want to go to sleep last night

even x-ing down and macrobiotic supper

                    in my stomach

and you too. and even fighting all that tired

my eyes pulled open and open, inverse of daylight

blinking. my eyes kept opening (and opening)

to see you

                cyriusplay@hotmail.tv

something like perfume the warmth and dampness at the back of your neck when waking, after a length of tendering my coughing, of getting water in the middle of the night and calling me a bed buffalo cuz i'd kept squeezing too tight up to you you were all the other side of the bed. wetness and heat at the top of your spine, base of your skull, mopping up a little in your hair... knocked me out.   flavour and taste overwhelming every other sense and sleep.

          20

but sometimes
i just feel like i'm on
> *the exit show*
of girls parading their various
> *flavours*
through your bedroom walls—
(and this all goes on video~
and i'm writing poems)

my hands callous watching you
move though / so many souls so lightly,
and quickly.

i've been wanting you for two weeks
and the girl on the couch with my shirt
up and the man on his side to my side
his shoulders so built, they are electricity
in these hands that reach toward your face.

    we all had something

                           one line

to say to each other

my line of fear is i will fall from grace
a fantasy of a girl who can not
live up to it; mouth just mouth
breasts on lips lips on breasts breast on lips and
tonight my best girl fell

straight down (an angel's
wings held together by glue too close to the sun)
fell back into her car and flew
            into the night

                        —fallen you, i
                        followed you—

4

my woman's walkin' slow
with the isle all full a' people
down it and outside where they paint
their nails and wear blood-red new boots / with buckles

3

he pads down into the underground to see
an ex from the heroin days. small and fit he
tucks in his shirt in a fashion-relic move from his youth
and he's looking, always looking—

and i don't know what happens after that
maybe his age catches up with him
like a train in a track

maybe he learns to breathe
and leaves off carrying the fishing-weights
as protection / he doesn't need / in the safer neighbourhoods he now inhabits

6

in the McD's drive through with the
bit of cobalt night pulling up the
drive *star light star bright even if you're*
a satellite i wish i may i wish i might
have the wish i wish tonight
    10-year-old boy laughed in the tin grey
11-year-old toyota— and we got him dinner

10 echo/shadow

because

        that your body is more frail with the anti-depressants

        and you can't cum

        that your days and nights are booked and i

        am not in there (those plans)—

        that we fall asleep, you in me, spooned

        that you are exactly the taste i crave

        and move through air as if it marks you or you it

        in your apartment, over furniture or standing (delicate as you do) or

              and/or if i get closer

              i'm just in for trouble

because you hoist yourself   along ridged lines of multiples, scanning the small box in the corn

        of the t.v. always looking for the next show.

        and i can fit, or not,

        but your structure doesn't breath for me

        doesn't bend or move / and i,

i run off like rain water

Coda:

sometimes one steps off, another steps in
i imagine that's what you think, this night
after first date with new bisexual lover
after a day of shopping and taking care of this
or that out and about before going into the city again or
after another lover in Marin or / adjusting the back
of one long ago finished.

i step off. others attract, random
scatter of pool balls on a break
where the table is suddenly alive with motion
then still

part 3: currency

don't know your phone # off by heart

don't know your friends / you slip from me like glue

as soon as you become a rock around my neck

i cut you off

i got trashed on you. each time

it took a few days to come back up

from the scud of belly-down under you

        you know where

          the edge lies. i know

        where it lies. an anxious

       precipice. a breath shortened

you don't want to deepen into

fall in and let go   you

want to hold it all at bay. restrain it lightly with silk ties

on a bed that holds you alone most nights

like pussy holds cock wrap't in rubber

though you didn't wash off me

like another man's cologne in a shower i want to believe

all it really took was metronidazole, zithromax, and fluconazole

to burn you outta me

raindrops on the clothesline hang
like christmas lights

my body is joined to yours under
                    my nails
the taste of the skin of your back.

Author Biography

Anne F. Walker's previous books of poetry include Into the Peculiar Dark, Pregnant Poems, and Six Months Rent. She founded Redwood Coast Press, and edited the anthology of poetry and poetic prose bite to eat place with Andrea Adolph. After earning a BFA from York University's Creative Writing Program in Toronto, she worked briefly in film, subsequently designing a program in Urban Poetics at the University of California, Berkeley. Her poetry has been granted awards from the Canada Council, the Ontario Arts Council, the Ontario Film Development Corporation, and the bpNichol Memorial Fund. Twice her work won the University of California's Eisner award for literature. A Canadian/ American dual national, she divides her time between Berkeley and Toronto.